Mountain Biking
the Twin Cities

Mountain Biking
the Twin Cities

STEVE JOHNSON

FALCON® Helena, Montana

*A*FALCON GUIDE ®

Falcon® Publishing is continually expanding its list of recreational guidebooks. All books include detailed descriptions, accurate maps, and all information necessary for enjoyable trips. You can order extra copies of this book and get information and prices for other Falcon books by writing Falcon, P.O. Box 1718, Helena, Montana 59624 or calling toll free 1-800-582-2665. Also, please ask for a free copy of our current catalog. Visit our website at www.FalconOutdoors.com or contact us by e-mail at falcon@falcon.com.

Library of Congress Cataloging-in-Publication Data

Johnson, Steve, 1965-
    Mountain biking the Twin Cities / by Steve Johnson.
        p.   cm. — (A Falcon guide)
    ISBN 1-56044-743-5 (pbk.)
    1. All terrain cycling—Minnesota—Mineapolis Metropolitan Area—
Guidebooks. 2. All terrain cycling—Minnesota—Saint Paul
Metropolitan Area—Guidebooks. 3. Minneapolis Metropolitan
Area (Minn.)—Guidebooks. 4. Saint Paul Metropolitan Area
(Minn.)—Guidebooks. I. Title II. Series
GV1045.5.M62M555   1999
917.76'5790453—dc21   98-54385
                                                                CIP

CAUTION

Outdoor recreational activities are by their very nature potentially hazardous. All participants in such activities must assume the responsibility for their own actions and safety. The information contained in this guidebook cannot re-place sound judgment and good decision-making skills, which help reduce risk exposure, nor does the scope of this book allow for disclosure of all the potential hazards and risks involved in such activities.

Learn as much as possible about the outdoor recreational activities in which you participate, prepare for the unexpected, and be cautious. The re-ward will be a safer and more enjoyable experience.

 Text pages printed on recycled paper.

For Mom and Dad—always there for us

Contents

Acknowledgments

I'd like to thank my wife most of all for enduring another summer of sunny afternoons alone while her husband was off wandering the woods "working" on this book.

Dr. James Work at Colorado State University continues to inspire me to pursue my passion for writing about my outdoor escapades. Thanks for the push.

John Burbidge at Falcon Publishing provided technical advice and pep talks throughout this project. Peggy O'Neill McLeod and Larissa Berry expertly polished it off and were always fun to work with.

And, thanks to Terry Williams at the City of Bloomington and everyone at the Minnesota Valley National Wildlife Refuge office for answers and suggestions on some of the popular river valley trails. I also had help from various bike shop employees and anonymous riders I met who offered hints and secrets on where to ride.

Preface

Sure, it sounds easy—just go find a few mountain bike trails and write a book about 'em. Alas, the trails in question are in and around a major metropolitan area with lots of cars and freeways and strip malls. How many decent rides could there be in such a place? And so the hunt began.

I ended the summer with a full limit of great fat tire trails. I played in familiar places where I grew up and discovered new locales that I didn't even know were out there. There was much rejoicing.

Minneapolis has been dubbed the City of Lakes, but it is much more than that. With its neighboring cities and towns, the Twin Cities are also home to a bevy of secluded parks and natural areas ideal for ducking away from the crowds and experiencing the wilderness close to home. It can be difficult to find quality places to take your mountain bike in a big city, but here are 21 rides for you to sample in your own backyard—romps through the river valley, city and county park loops, the solitude of a wildlife refuge, and even a ski area.

This book highlights mountain biking as it was meant to be: off the road and in the dirt. With the exception of a couple of—gasp!—paved routes, all the trails you'll see here are down and dirty. You can cruise along the flat LRT trail or cough up your lungs on the hills at Murphy-Hanrehan or Afton Alps. It's also nice to take in the "beauteeful" fall colors along the Cannon Valley trail. (Hey, a little paved riding ain't gonna hurt ya.)

If you're a local here, I hope this book guides you to some undiscovered stashes of riding or ignites some enthusiasm for an old favorite. If you are visiting or are new to the area, grab your bike and get to know us.

I'll look for you on the trails!

Steve Johnson
Roaming the Minnesota River Valley, September, 1998

MAP LEGEND

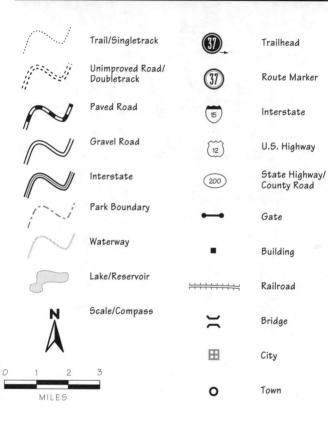

Trail/Singletrack	Trailhead
Unimproved Road/Doubletrack	Route Marker
Paved Road	Interstate
Gravel Road	U.S. Highway
Interstate	State Highway/County Road
Park Boundary	Gate
Waterway	Building
Lake/Reservoir	Railroad
Scale/Compass	Bridge
N	City
0 1 2 3 MILES	Town

Twin City Metro Area

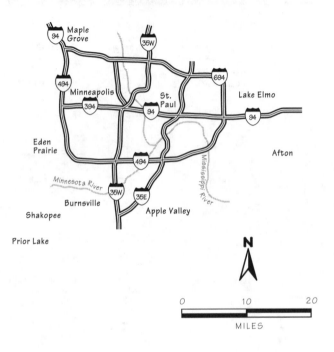

River Valley Area

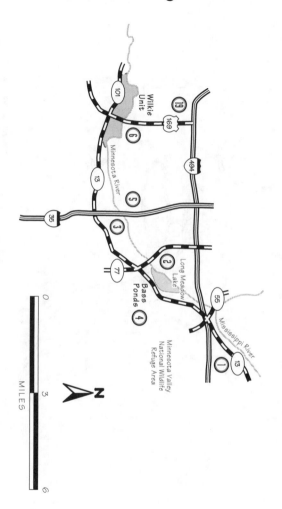

West-Southwest Metro Area

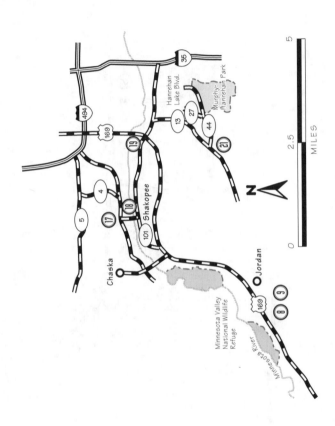

East-Northwest Metro Area

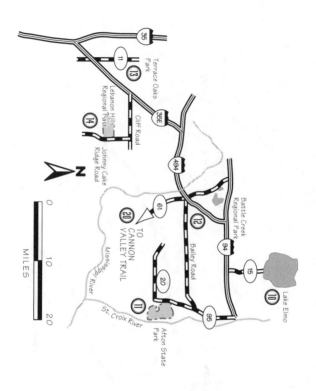

Northwest Metro Area

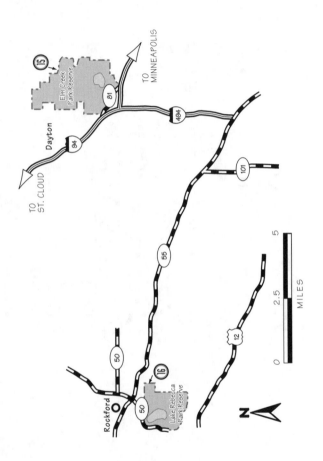

Get Ready to CRANK!

I stared blankly at my map for a half-hour again this morning trying to discover a worthy route I could turn the pedals on. This is a familiar scene for many mountain bikers, especially those who live in an urban area and have limited choices to begin with. If you're new to the area, where can you go to ride? Where can you even look to locate a trail? If you are a long-time local, how do you avoid the customary pilgrimage to the same old trails week after week? If only there was a way to find new challenging terrain and areas that are fat-tire friendly, or to find a place to just roll along and enjoy the sights when you're not in the mood for a hammerfest.

Welcome to *Mountain Biking the Twin Cities.* Here are 21+ rides ranging from easy paved paths to smooth singletrack to steep, rock-strewn hills and remote river valleys. The rides are described in plain language, with accurate distances and ratings for physical and technical difficulty. Each entry offers a wealth of detailed information that's easy to read and use, from your couch or on the trail.

Our aim is threefold: to help you choose a ride that's appropriate for fitness and skill level; to make it easy to find the trailhead; and to help you complete the ride in one piece, without getting lost. Take care of these basics and big fun is bound to break loose.

The Twin Cities Area: What to Expect

The rides in this book cover a wide variety of terrain. Many of the routes begin innocently enough on pavement or smooth gravel, then change to steep, rutted paths littered with rocks. Certain details of your preparations for an easy spin on a road route or even a dirt bike path will be quite a bit different than for an extended tour deep into the woods.

In some areas of the Twin Cities, the terrain can change drastically from one mile to the next. It is important to be ready for those changes before you ride. Put in plenty of miles on your bike to get in good shape ahead of time, and know your limits. Clean rims, brakes, handlebars, seat, shifters, derailleurs, and chain to make sure they survived the last trip and are functioning properly. Get into this habit after your ride, also. There's lots of mud on many of the low-lying routes here and your bike will thank you if you clean the goop off before it ruins bearings, cogs, and other important parts.

A helmet is essential for mountain biking; it can save your life and prevent serious injuries. My face landed on a log one day, and thanks to my helmet I left the scene with only a big knot on my head instead of taking a stroll through the Pearly Gates. Don't ride without one. Cycling gloves are another indispensable piece of safety equipment that can save hands from cuts and bruises from falls, encroaching branches, and rocks. They also improve your grip and comfort on the handlebars.

Always pack or carry at least one full water bottle. On longer rides, don't leave the house without two (or even three) bottles, or plan your ride so it passes someplace where potable water is available. A snack such as fruit or energy bars can keep those huge quads cranking for extra hours and prevent the dreaded "bonk"—the sudden loss of energy when your body runs out of fuel. Dress for the weather, and pack a jacket that repels both wind and water in case the weather turns ugly. Don't forget sunglasses, sunscreen (use the sports stuff that won't run down into your eyes and mouth), lip balm, and insect repellent, which is especially critical in mid-summer when riding by a swamp.

A basic tool kit can save you from a long walk or even a dark night out in the woods. A tire pump and tube patch kit are vital, and a few other tools can make the difference between disaster and a five-minute pit stop. Carry a set of Allen wrenches or an all-in-one tool for tightening or adjusting seat post, handlebars, chainrings, pedals, brake posts, and other components. While I generally carry just a minimum, some folks aren't comfortable unless they bring a whole shop's worth of tools. They're weighted down and wrenches rattle with every bump in the trail, but they are rarely stranded by mechanical failures.

This book is designed to be easily carried in a jersey pocket or bike bag, and the maps and ride descriptions will help anyone unfamiliar with the trails. U.S. Geological Survey (USGS) topographic maps can provide a more detailed view of the terrain, but most ride routes in this book are not shown. I have listed some of the clearest and most easily attainable maps for each ride.

Minnesota's weather spans a wide range of extremes, particularly in early spring and late fall. Snow has been known to linger well into April, and 40 inches piled up in October recently. If you're really dedicated (or nuts), it is possible to get some riding in during the winter. However, keep in mind that Minneapolis is the coldest major city on the planet, and don't be surprised to see the mercury drop to minus 50 degrees F! Summer highs can climb above 100 degrees F and be laced with stifling humidity. During most of the season, however, the climate is pleasant. Riding conditions are usually at their finest from early June to mid-October. Spring weather or heavy summer rains may make parts or all of some trails unridable.

Also keep in mind that special hunting seasons may take place in the Minnesota River valley and overlap the riding season. If riding in an area with bullets flying, don't wear your moose antler bike helmet. Wear blaze orange and check with the Department of Natural Resources for specific hunting dates (see Appendix B). Hard rains and late or early snow can turn trails into mud consommé for days. ("Hey waiter, there's a spoke in my soup!") This is especially prevalent on the river valley trails, which flood often and easily. Please stay off wet, muddy trails—the soil damage and erosion even one rider can cause is simply too great, and a damaged trail often becomes a closed trail.

In general, most of these metro trails remain ridable throughout the season. Use your noggin and plan ahead before heading out. Most rides in this book have hotlines or contact numbers to use to receive updates on current trail conditions (see Appendix B for information sources).

Rules of the Trail

I can hear you grumbling. "Oh, great," you're thinking. "Here's another yahoo telling us how we should ride." Relax. The rules of the trail are merely reminders to all riders that taking care of the trails and being courteous to your fellow trail users helps to keep our favorite rides open and in great shape.

If every mountain biker always yielded the right-of-way, stayed on the trail, avoided wet or muddy trails, never cut through a meadow, always rode in control, showed respect for other trail users, and carried out every last scrap of what was carried in (Power Bar wrappers, destroyed tubes, etc.)—if we all just—we wouldn't need a list of rules governing our sport. Fact is, most mountain bikers are conscientious and are trying to do the right thing. Most of us own that integrity. (No one becomes good at something as demanding and painful as grunting up steep ridges by cheating.) Most of us don't need rules. But we do need knowledge of what exactly is the right thing to do.

Here are some guidelines (friendly reminders) reprinted by permission from the International Mountain Bicycling Association (IMBA). The basic idea is to prevent or avoid conflicts with other backcountry visitors and users. Ride with respect.

IMBA Rules of the Trail

Thousands of miles of dirt trails have been closed to mountain bicyclists. The irresponsible riding habits of a few riders have been a factor. Do your part to maintain trail access by observing the following rules of the trail, formulated by the IMBA. IMBA's mission is to promote environmentally sound and socially responsible mountain biking.

1. Ride on open trails only. Respect trail and road closures (ask if not sure), avoid possible trespass on private land, obtain permits and authorization as may be required. Federal and state wilderness areas are closed to cycling. The way you ride will influence trail management decisions and policies.

2. Leave no trace. Be sensitive to the dirt beneath you. Even on open (legal) trails, you should not ride under conditions where you will leave evidence of your passing, such as on certain soils after a rain. Recognize different types of soil and trail construction; practice low-impact cycling. (Ride softly and carry a big...pump.) This also means staying on existing trails and not creating any new ones. Be sure to pack out at least as much as you pack in.

3. Control your bicycle! Inattention for even a second can cause problems. Obey all bicycle speed regulations and recommendations.

4. Always yield trail. Make known your approach well in advance. A friendly greeting (or bell) is considerate and works well; don't startle others. Show your respect when passing by slowing to a walking pace or stopping. Anticipate other trail users at corners and blind spots.

5. Never spook animals. All animals are startled by an un-announced approach, a sudden movement, or a loud noise. This can be dangerous for you, others, and the animals. Give animals extra room and time to adjust to you. When passing horses use special care and follow directions from the horse-back riders (dismount and ask if uncertain). Running cattle and disturbing wildlife is a serious offense. Leave gates as you found them, or as marked.

6. Plan ahead. Know your equipment, your ability, and the area in which you are riding—and prepare accordingly. Be self-sufficient at all times, keep your equipment in good repair, and carry necessary supplies for changes in weather or other conditions. A well-executed trip is a satisfaction to you and not a burden or offense to others. Always wear a helmet.

Keep trails open by setting a good example of environmentally sound and socially responsible off-road cycling.

How to Use this Guide

Mountain Biking the Twin Cities describes 21 mountain bike rides in their entirety. A handful of additional routes in the area are mentioned briefly in Appendix A. Many of the featured rides are loops, beginning and ending at the same point but coming and going on different trails. Loops are by far the most popular type of ride, and this book has bunches of 'em. Be forewarned, however: the difficulty of a loop ride may change dramatically depending on which direction you ride around the loop. If you are unfamiliar with the rides in this book, try them first as described here. The directions follow the path of least resistance (which does not necessarily mean easy). After you've been over the terrain, you can determine whether a given loop would be fun—or even imaginable—in the reverse direction.

Portions of some rides follow gravel or paved roads, and others never even see a road. Purists may wince at rides on paved roads or bike paths in a book about mountain biking, but these are special rides. They offer a chance to enjoy the forest and fresh air while covering easier, non-technical terrain for people new to the sport. They can also be used by hard-core riders on "active rest" days or when other trails are closed or too wet.

Each ride description in this book follows the same format:

Number and name of the ride: Rides are cross-referenced by number throughout this book. In many cases, parts of rides or entire routes can be linked to other rides for longer trips or variations on a standard route. These opportunities are noted. For some of the names of rides I relied on official names of trails, roads, and natural features as shown on USGS, and park maps. Some of them I just made up. In some cases, signs or trail markers in the field may show slightly different names.

Location: The general whereabouts of the ride; distance and direction from nearest town.

Distance: The length of the ride in miles, given as a loop, one way, or round trip.

Time: An estimate of how long it takes to complete the ride, for example: 1 to 2 hours. *The time listed is the actual riding time and does not include rest stops.* Strong, skilled riders may be able to do a given ride in less than the estimated time, while other riders may take considerably longer. Also bear in mind that severe weather, changes in trail conditions, or mechanical problems may prolong a ride.

Tread: The type of road or trail: paved road, gravel road, dirt road or jeep track, doubletrack, ATV-width singletrack, and singletrack.

Aerobic level: The level of physical effort required to complete the ride: easy, moderate, or strenuous. (See explanation of the rating system on page 11).

Technical difficulty: The level of bike handling skills needed to complete the ride upright and in one piece. Technical difficulty is rated on a scale from 1 to 5, with 1 being the easiest and 5 the hardest. (See explanation of the rating system on page 12.)

Hazards: A list of dangers that may be encountered on a ride, including traffic, weather, trail obstacles and conditions, risky stream crossings, obscure trails, and other perils. Remember: conditions may change at any time. Be alert for storms, new fences, downfall, missing trail signs, and mechanical failure. Fatigue, heat, cold, and/or dehydration may impair judgment. Always wear a helmet and other safety equipment. Ride in control at all times.

Highlights: Special features or qualities that make a ride worth doing (as if we needed an excuse!): scenery, fun singletrack, chances to see wildlife.

Land status: A list of managing agencies or landowners. Many of the rides in this book are part of the Minnesota Valley National Wildlife Refuge (U.S. Fish and Wildlife Service). But many of the rides also cross portions of private, state, county, or municipal lands. Do not enter areas where riding isn't allowed. And respect the land, regardless of who owns it. See Appendix B for a list of local addresses for land-managing agencies. **Stay on the trail or stay home.**

Maps: A list of available maps. A good state map or the Minnesota Gazetteer will provide a good overview of the Twin Cities area and show some elevation intervals. USGS topographic maps in the 0.5-minute quad series provide a close-up look at terrain, but few of these rides are shown. Also check Bureau of Land Management 1:100,000 maps for additional outlooks on the area. Not all routes are shown on official maps; in fact, some of the rides follow unmapped routes. For these particular rides the map in this book may be the only map available. Beware of the urge to ride on every spur trail you see as many will lead to a dead-end or onto private land.

Access: How to find the trailhead or start of the ride. A number of rides begin right from a town; for others it's best to drive to the trailhead.

The ride: A mile-by-mile list of key points—landmarks, notable climbs and descents, stream crossings, obstacles, hazards, major turns and junctions—along the ride. All distances were measured to the tenth of a mile with a cyclo-computer (a bike-mounted odometer). Terrain, riding technique, and even tire pressure can affect odometer readings, so treat all mileages as estimates.

Finally, one last reminder that the real world is changing all the time. The information presented here is as accurate and up-to-date as possible, but there are no guarantees out in the woods. You alone are responsible for your safety and for the choices you make on the trail.

If you do find an error or omission in this book, or a new and noteworthy change in the field, I'd like to hear from you. Please write to Steve Johnson, c/o Falcon Publishing, P.O. Box 1718, Helena, MT 59624.

Rating the Rides: One Person's Pain is Another's Pleasure

One of the first lessons learned by most mountain bikers is to not trust their friends' accounts of how easy or difficult a given ride may be.

"Where ya wanna ride today?"

"Let's just go easy, maybe cruise the valley or somethin'. I've hardly been on the bike at all, don't feel too strong."

If you don't read between the lines, only painful experience will tell you that your buddy eats intervals for breakfast and hammers five-hour training rides "just to get the heart rate up."

So how do you know what you're getting into, before it's too late? Don't always listen to your friends, especially right at the start of a ride. But do read this book. FalconGuides rate each ride for two types of difficulty: the physical effort required to pedal the distance, and the level of bike handling skills needed to stay vertical and make it home in one piece. We call these *Aerobic Level and Technical Difficulty.*

The following sections explain what the various ratings mean in plain, specific language. Also weigh other factors such as elevation gain, total trip distance, weather and wind, and current trail conditions.

Aerobic Level Ratings

Bicycling is often touted as a relaxing, low-impact, relatively easy way to burn excess calories and maintain a healthy heart and lungs. Mountain biking, however, tends to pack a little more work (and excitement) into the routine.

Fat tires and soft or rough trails increase the rolling resistance, so it takes more effort to push those wheels around. Unpaved and off-road hills are often steeper than grades measured and tarred by the highway department. When we use the word *steep*, we mean a sweat-inducing, oxygen-sucking, lactose-building climb. If it's followed by an exclamation point—steep!—expect some real pain on the way up (and maybe for days afterward). So expect to breathe hard and sweat some, probably a lot. Pedaling around town is a good start, but it won't fully prepare you for the workout offered by most of the rides in this book. If you're unsure of your level of fitness, see a doctor for a physical exam before tackling any of these rides. And if you're riding to get back in shape or just for the fun of it, take it easy. Walk or rest if need be. Start with short rides and add miles gradually.

Here's how we rate the exertion level for terrain covered in this book:

Easy: Flat or gently rolling terrain. No steep or prolonged climbs.

Moderate: Some hills. Climbs may be short and fairly steep or long and gradual.

Strenuous: Frequent or prolonged climbs steep enough to require riding in the lowest gear; requires a high level of aerobic fitness, power, endurance, and grunting (all typically acquired through many hours of riding and proper training). Less fit riders may need to walk.

Many rides are mostly easy or moderate but may have short strenuous sections. Other rides are mostly strenuous and should be attempted only after a complete medical checkup and implant of a second heart, preferably a *big* one. Also be aware that flailing through a highly technical section can be exhausting even on the flats. Good riding skills and a relaxed stance on the bike save energy.

Finally, any ride can be strenuous if you ride it hard and fast. Conversely, the pain of a lung-burning climb grows easier to tolerate as your fitness level improves. Learn to pace yourself and schedule easy rides and rest days into your calendar.

Technical Difficulty Ratings

While you're pushing up that steep, rocky slope, wondering how much farther you can go before your lungs prolapse and billow out of your mouth like an air bag in a desperate gasp for oxygen, remember that the dry heaves aren't the only hurdle on the way to the top of the hill. There's that tree across the trail, or the sideslope littered with marble-sized pebbles, or the place where the trail disappears except for tiny pieces of Lycra clinging to the outstretched limbs of a thieving oak tree.

Mountain bikes will roll over or through an amazing array of life's little challenges, but sometimes we, as riders, have to help. Or at least close our eyes and hang on. As a last resort, some riders get off their bikes and walk—get this—*before* they flip over the handlebars. These folks have no sense of adventure. The rest of us hop onto our bikes with only the dimmest inkling of what lies ahead. Later we brag about the Ride from Hell (leaving out the part about carrying our bikes over much of that hellish terrain).

No more. The technical difficulty ratings in this book help take the worst surprises out of backcountry rides. In the privacy of your own home you can make an honest appraisal of your bike handling skills and then find rides in these pages that match your ability.

We rate technical difficulty on a scale from 1 to 5 (1 being easiest). We tried to make the ratings as objective as possible by considering the type and frequency of the ride's obstacles. The same standards were applied consistently through all the rides in the book.

We've also added plus (+) and minus (-) symbols to cover gray area between given levels of difficulty: a 4+ obstacle is harder than a 4, but easier than a -5. A stretch of trail rated as 5+ would be unridable by all but the most skilled (or luckiest) riders.

Here are the five levels defined:

Level 1: Smooth tread; road or doubletrack; no obstacles, ruts, or steeps. Requires basic bike riding skills.

Level 2: Mostly smooth tread; wide, well-groomed singletrack or road/doubletrack with minor ruts or loose gravel or sand.

Level 3: Irregular tread with some rough sections; single or doubletrack with obvious route choices; some steep sections; occasional obstacles may include small rocks, roots, water bars, ruts, loose gravel or sand, and sharp turns.

Level 4: Rough tread with few smooth places; singletrack or rough doubletrack with limited route choices; steep sections, some with obstacles; obstacles are numerous and varied, including rocks, roots, branches, ruts, sidehills, narrow tread, loose gravel or sand, and sharp turns.

Level 5: Continuously broken, rocky, root-infested, or trenched tread; singletrack or extremely rough doubletrack with few route choices; frequent, sudden, and severe changes in gradient; some slopes so steep that wheels lift off ground; obstacles are nearly continuous and may include boulders, logs, water, large holes, deep ruts, ledges, piles of loose gravel, steep sidehills, encroaching trees, and really sharp turns.

Again, most of the rides in this book cover varied terrain, with an ever-changing degree of difficulty. Some trails run smooth with only occasional obstacles and others are seemingly all one big obstacle. The path of least resistance, or *line*, is where you find it. In general, most obstacles are more challenging if you encounter them while climbing than while descending. On the other hand, in heavy surf (e.g., long sections of boulders, tangles of downfall, deep sand), fear plays a larger role when facing downhill. Realize, too, that different riders have different strengths and weaknesses. Some folks can scramble over logs and boulders without a grunt, but they crash head over sprocket at every sharp, sandy turn. Some fly off the steepest drops and others freeze. Some riders climb like the wind and others just blow...and walk.

The key to overcoming "technical difficulties" is practice: keep trying. Follow a rider who makes it look easy, and don't hesitate to ask for constructive criticism. Try shifting your weight (good riders move a lot, front to back, side to side, and up and down) and experimenting with balance and momentum. Find a smooth patch of lawn and practice riding as slowly as possible, even balancing at a standstill in a "track stand" (described in the Glossary). This will give you more confidence—and more time to recover or bail out—the next time the trail rears up and bites.

Mendota Trail

Location: Along south side of Minnesota River adjacent to Minnesota Highway 13 between Minnesota Highway 55 and Interstate 494.

Distance: 8.7 miles, out and back.

Time: 25–45 minutes.

Tread: 0.4 mile on pavement; remaining 8.3 miles on wide gravel trail.

Aerobic level: Easy.

Technical difficulty: 1 on entire trail.

Hazards: Some loose gravel to watch for in places.

Highlights: Great beginner ride or easy spin on flat terrain. Fun ride along the river flats.

Land status: Fort Snelling State Park.

Maps: State park brochures.

Access: Begin at parking area on MN 13 just west of Sibley Historic Site and town of Mendota, near MN 110 and 55.

The ride

0.0   Ride east toward Mendota on sidewalk next to

Mendota Trail

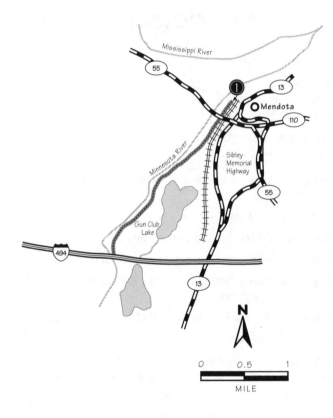

Minnesota's oldest European-American settlement with 1800's-era limestone houses. Go left on Water Street and curve down past the Sibley house. Turn right under the railroad trestle and into Fort Snelling State Park. The Minnesota River is right in front of you. The confluence of the Minnesota and the Mississippi rivers is to the east. Some of us call this section the Minnihippi River. Take the trail to the left, riding underneath MN 55.

1.2 Trail bends away from the bluff and into heavily wooded river flats. Huge cottonwoods, elms, maple, and ash trees live here. Trail is a flat, relatively wide gravel road.

2.2 Cross cement bridge over drainage from the river's flood plain. (Watch for herons.) The structure above and to your right is the airport's strobe beacon for inbound planes.

3.1 Pass under I-494 bridge. (It is possible to ride past the cement bridge columns and clamber up the opposite bank to a paved bike trail that leads to Bloomington or Eagan.) This ride reverses at this point and returns on the trail to Mendota.

8.7 Trailhead.

Fort Snelling State Park

Location: Along south bank of Minnesota River between Interstate 494 and Cedar Avenue.

• Fort Snelling State
   Park Trail

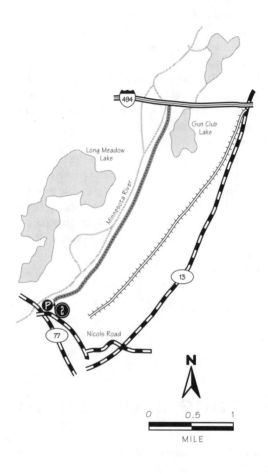

Distance: Approximately 4 miles, out and back.

Time: 15–30 minutes.

Tread: A mix of wide gravel and dirt singletrack and mud.

Aerobic level: Easy+.

Technical difficulty: 2, with sections of 1 on either end of the trail.

Hazards: Some roots and rocks to negotiate; gooey mud after a rain.

Highlights: A fun and scenic ride along the river through thick woods and marsh land.

Land status: Ft. Snelling State Park.

Maps: State park brochures.

Access: This ride is best started from the Cedar Avenue bike ramp and boat landing. From the south, take Silver Bell Road north from Minnesota Highway 13 to Nichols Road. Follow this road to the parking area underneath the Cedar Avenue Bridge. The trail begins at the base of the bike ramp heading east.

Note: This route offers easy access to Ride 1. Many people combine these two routes into one longer ride; they are separated in this book to highlight each ride's features.

The ride

0.0 Begin riding east at the base of the bike ramp, following a dirt trail through the trees. A sign with a map of the park is posted on your left as you continue on to a wider, gravel trail.

0.7 Cross a wooden bridge and a small creek. Trail narrows and turns to hard-packed dirt on the other side of bridge. Ride into area heavily wooded with silver maple and cottonwood trees. This section gets very soft and sticky when wet. Best to avoid this trail altogether after a rain to limit damage.

0.8 Cross a second wooden bridge.

0.9 Cross another wooden bridge, and ride into bush-wacking country. As this book went to press, the board-walk-style bridge through this area was still out, washed away during a high-water spring. No word yet on the completion date of a new bridge. When it stays dry for an extended period, you can keep riding through the swamp on hard-packed mud, following whichever trail you like and finally reaching the turnaround point. However, even a light rain turns this section into an oozing, pulsating, bike-eating pit of no return. Do not dare to test the Swamp Thing.

2.1 Junction with Interstate 494 Bridge and Ride 1. Do a U-turn and ride back west.

4.2 Trailhead.

River Valley Rover

Location: Along the Minnesota River bluff and wetland area between Cedar Avenue and Interstate 35 West.

Distance: 9.3-mile loop.

Time: 1.25 to 1.5 hours.

• River Valley Rover

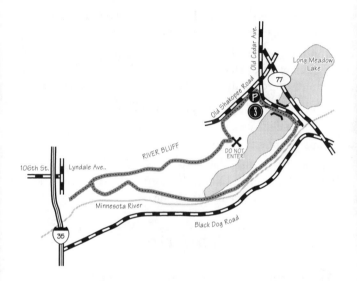

Long Meadow Lake

Old Cedar Ave.

Old Shakopee Road

77

P

3

DO NOT ENTER

RIVER BLUFF

106th St.

Lyndale Ave..

Minnesota River

35

Black Dog Road

N

0   0.5   1

MILE

Tread: 6.1 miles dirt singletrack, 3.2 miles paved road.

Aerobic level: A little of each—easy to strenuous.

Technical difficulty: 1 on early sections of trail, 2–3+ through middle portion, 4 on last stretches of trail before the paved road.

Hazards: Deep, loose sand; sticky mud if wet; several stream crossings; carnivorous mosquitoes.

Highlights: Fun ride along riverbank, then sweet, rolling singletrack through the bluff woods. Challenging climbs and a couple of screamin' downhills on well-maintained trail.

Land status: U.S. Fish and Wildlife Service; City of Bloomington.

Maps: Map in this book.

Access: Begin this loop at the parking area at bottom of the Old Cedar Avenue hill on the north side of the river. Ride across bridge to reach start of ride.

The ride

0.0 Ride an old bridge across the channel between the larger sections of Long Meadow Lake. Imagine quieter days when this was the bridge carrying auto traffic to the southern communities as you look to your left at the present-day exodus.

0.7 The road ends abruptly at the edge of the river. To your left is a bike ramp leading to the other side, to your right is a wide gravel trail. Go right. The trail follows along the riverbank and narrows to hard-packed dirt singletrack.

1.9 Pass the Black Dog power plant on south side of river. Ride through a stand of baby aspen and willow brush. Watch for loose sand in spots.

2.0–3.2 Lots of loose, deep sand to negotiate and some whoop-dee-doo's.

3.3 Bear right to avoid riding into a channel of the river. Ride along until you find a place to cross the channel to the other side (several options exist depending on trail conditions and your confidence level). Your goal is to get back to the main trail at the riverbank.

4.5 Stream crossing, then navigate through deadfall until trail reappears away from river.

4.6 Junction with main bluff trail. Lyndale Avenue is 0.42 mile down the left fork, Bloomington city streets are up the trail straight ahead, and you're going to the right. Climb on hard-packed dirt and point yourself east back toward Cedar Avenue.

5.2 Steep climb with deep sand. Use your strongest legs to get to the top.

5.4 Stream crossing.

5.5 Take the low road.

6.0 You made it to higher ground at Parker's Picnic Grounds with great views of the valley. Follow the trail back down a steep hill; use caution.

6.4 Steep climb to Quinn's Point.

6.6 Take the right fork back down the hill. Turn and ride up again past the Minnesota Valley National Wildlife Refuge sign. **Do not ride into the refuge at this point. Bikes are not allowed between here and Cedar Avenue. Stay on the trail or stay home.** Don't be tempted by the tracks of ruffians who have ignored the rules. Keep climbing up to Indian Mounds Park on Eleventh Avenue. Follow Eleventh Avenue north, working your way to Old Shakopee Road. Take Old Shakopee Road east to...

8.8 Old Cedar Avenue. Go right and down the hill to the parking area.

9.3 Trailhead.

Bass Ponds Loop

Location: On the north side of the Minnesota River immediately east of Cedar Avenue.

Distance: 3.2-mile loop.

Time: 15–25 minutes.

Tread: Entire loop is on medium to wide gravel trail.

Aerobic level: Easy.

Technical difficulty: 1 on entire trail, with one section of stairs to hike up.

Hazards: Occasional loose gravel; slippery goose droppings.

Highlights: Relaxed ride through wildlife-abundant area near river; great beginner loop.

Land status: U.S. Fish and Wildlife Service.

Maps: Refuge brochures.

Access: Start this ride at the north end of the old Cedar Avenue Bridge, about a half-mile south of Old Shakopee Road in Bloomington. Easy access from Minnesota Highway 77 just to the east.

The ride

0.0 Ride across the road, past the gate, and onto a wide gravel trail heading east toward the highway. This is a

• Bass Ponds Loop Trail

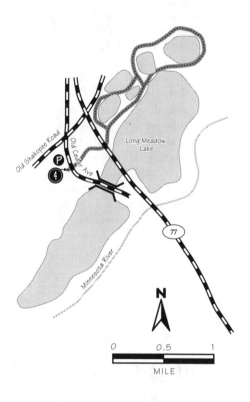

Old Shakopee Road

Old Cedar Ave

P

4

Long Meadow Lake

Minnesota River

77

N

0   0.5   1
MILE

very popular trail for hikers and birdwatchers. Respect their space. Control your speed.

0.5 Ride under MN 77 through a tricky section of dirt trail. Use caution. Immediately after the bridge you will need to hike your bike up a short stairway leading up from the river. Continue east on the path, riding along the Hog Back Ridge Pond. These ponds were created for rearing bass by the Izaak Walton League in 1926. The ponds remained in operation for over 30 years, and were eventually sold to the U.S. Fish and Wildlife Service.

1.3 Junction with trail to Big Bass Pond; turn right. Ride across a finely-crafted wooden bridge and lean to the right. Ride slowly through this section and be on the lookout for wildlife of all kinds; water, forest, and wetland areas make for deluxe accommodations for mallards, chipmunks, or bald eagles.

1.7 Continue riding past the wooden bridge to your right. Ride past the parking area and information kiosks (after stopping to read a little background information on the ponds) and back toward the trailhead. Choose a different pond and explore this small but unique area.

3.2 Trailhead.

Bloomington Ferry Trail

Location: Along the north banks of Minnesota River between Interstate 35 and the old Bloomington Ferry Bridge (County Road 18).

Distance: 13.7 miles, out and back.

Time: 1.25 to 1.75 hours.

Tread: 12.8 miles dirt singletrack; 0.9 mile wide gravel trail.

Aerobic level: Moderate+.

Technical difficulty: 2 on gravel portion of trail; 3+ on all singletrack sections.

Hazards: Loose sand; inlets from river to cross; technical log crossings; hike-a-bike sections to and from the raft. Area is prone to flooding; avoid riding after heavy rain.

Highlights: Long, challenging singletrack ride next to the river. Well-maintained trail that tests your handling skills and offers some of the best scenery in the valley.

Land status: City of Bloomington; U.S. Fish and Wildlife Service.

Maps: Map in this book.

Access: This out and back route begins at the parking area on the north side of the old Bloomington Ferry Bridge. Access from Bloomington Ferry and Auto Club roads, or ride across from the south on a newer bike/hike path. Trail heads off from the left corner of the parking lot as you ride toward the bridge.

The ride

0.0 Ride toward bridge and off of the pavement onto the dirt trail. Use caution on this relatively steep descent and watch for bike-swallowing erosion gullies. Enter immediately into heavily-wooded flood plain area. This trail is shared with hikers. Ride smart.

1.7 Stream crossing through a ravine. Be alert for roots in the trail, along with downed logs and trees.

• Bloomington Ferry Trail

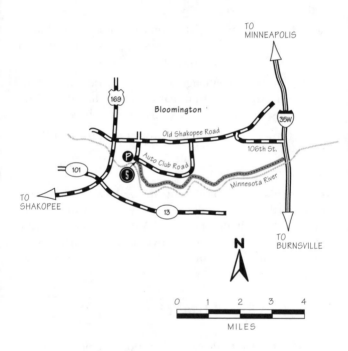

TO
MINNEAPOLIS

169

Bloomington

Old Shakopee Road

35W

106th St.

P

Auto Club Road

101

S

Minnesota River

TO
SHAKOPEE

13

N

TO
BURNSVILLE

| 0 | 1 | 2 | 3 | 4 |

MILES

2.3 Cross a stream over a handmade cairn of logs and sticks. Use caution.

2.6 Ride past grain elevators and barge operations across the river. Trail along here hugs the edge of the bank; don't lean too far to the right.

3.2 Pass under the old swinging bridge river crossing for auto traffic and trains.

3.3 Go over another log/stick stream crossing, and then another after that.

3.5 Yet another log bridge over a stream. How are your technical skills holding up?

5.0 The loose sand starts in this area. Power through it!

5.2 Wide stream crossing. A handy barrel raft is usually available for you to get over to the other side. Scramble carefully down and onto the raft, grab the rope that has been soaking in dirty, smelly water and pull yourself along, humming the "Dueling Banjoes" theme from *Deliverance* as you go. Use much caution getting on and off the raft. If you do start to sink into the goo, at least make sure your bike makes it out O.K.

6.1 Trail evolves into a wide, hard-packed gravel path, then a wider service road. Follow this all the way to the I-35 West Bridge.

6.9 Arrive at the freeway bridge. There is access to Ride 3 right over there on the far side of the Lyndale Avenue parking area. This route turns around here and heads back west.

13.7 Trailhead.

New Bridge Trail

Location: On the north side of the Minnesota River riding west from County Road 18 (old Ferry Bridge). This trail passes underneath the "new" Bloomington Ferry Bridge, hence the trail's unimaginative name. The new bridge is already several years old, but we locals are in the habit of calling it new to distinguish it from the old one.

Distance: 2.2 miles, out and back.

Time: 10–15 minutes.

Tread: 1.4 miles gravel trail; 2 miles on dirt and grass.

Aerobic level: Easy.

Technical difficulty: 1–2 on entire trail.

Hazards: Maybe some loose sand or a deer crossing your path.

Highlights: Easy access trail through wooded river flats; study the construction of a freeway bridge.

Land status: U.S. Fish and Wildlife Service; City of Bloomington.

Maps: Map in this book.

Access: Park in same lot as Ride 5 and ride west on wide gravel trail.

• New Bridge Trail

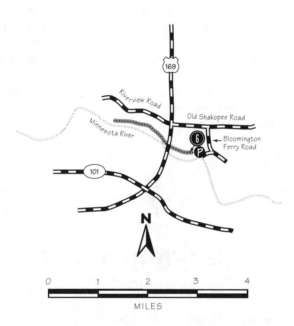

169

Riverview Road

Old Shakopee Road

Minnesota River

6
P
← Bloomington Ferry Road

101

N

| 0 | 1 | 2 | 3 | 4 |

MILES

The ride

0.0 Begin riding westbound from parking lot on wide gravel trail. This was a heavily-used access road during construction of the new river bridge.

0.7 Arrive directly underneath the recently completed Ferry Bridge. Admire the handiwork of yet another epic construction project, then continue on the trail along the riverbank. Trail turns to hard-packed dirt as it enters forested river flats. If you decide to take a right turn under the bridge, you will follow the northbound traffic flow and ride into a small pond/floodplain.

1.1 Trail enters large, open field. This is private property. Turn around and go back.

2.2 Trailhead.

St. Lawrence Unit
(wet side)

Location: Approximately 4 miles southwest of Jordan on the north side of U.S. Highway 169.

Distance: 4.4-mile loop.

Time: 18–30 minutes.

Tread: 0.5 mile gravel road; 3.9 miles grass and dirt trail.

Aerobic level: Moderate.

Technical difficulty: 1 on gravel road; 2 and 3 on trail.

• St. Lawrence Unit Trail
(wet side)

• St. Lawrence Unit Trail
(dry side)

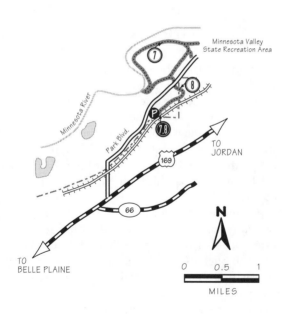

Hazards: Really bumpy sections early and late in ride; possible flooding when wet.

Highlights: Extremely quiet; scenic ride through river flats and historic town site.

Land status: State of Minnesota.

Maps: Map at park office.

Access: Drive 4 miles south of Jordan on US 169 to Park Boulevard. Turn right, cross the railroad tracks, and proceed to the park headquarters. Pay daily fee and, if office is staffed, inquire about parking. I started this ride at the park office, but alternate starting points are available on the way in.

The ride

0.0 Ride north (turn right) from the park office on the gravel road until you arrive at...

0.2 A wide, grassy trail that leads from both sides of the road; turn left. Hikers and horses also use this trail; be sure to yield to them. Go straight (lean left) at the first fork you come to. Trail starts out very bumpy, reminiscent of the Little Prairie Loop in Ride 8, and then blends with forested dirt path with the river over to your right.

0.7 Fork in the road. A left will dump you onto the gravel road you came in on, so take a right here. A map is posted on a sign for assistance. Trail descends a bit and snakes through two small ponds. Stop here and commune with nature. Only the faint drone of traffic ruins an otherwise idyllic setting.

1.3 Pass campground on your left.

1.6 This is the Trail Center. Picnic tables and an open area can be found here, as well as maps and information.

Continuing straight ahead will take you to Belle Plaine; this ride turns right and loops back toward the river. At the T intersection, take a right. Rough trail here with lots o' horse tracks and deep sand. Be ready.

3.7 Go straight at this fork, passing by historic site of town of St. Lawrence. Turn right when trail meets gravel road and continue back to the park office.

4.4 Park office and trailhead.

St. Lawrence Unit
(dry side)

Location: Same as Ride 7.

Distance: 1.3-mile loop.

Time: Approximately 10 minutes.

Tread: 0.4 mile gravel road; 0.9 mile rolling, grassy trail.

Aerobic level: Easy.

Technical difficulty: 1 on gravel road; 2 on grassy trail.

Hazards: A possible deep bump or two, otherwise this is a pretty tame trail.

Highlights: Fun ride through unique river valley ecosystem with aged oaks and thick sumac groves.

Land status: State of Minnesota.

Maps: Park maps.

Access: See Ride 7.

0.0 Begin ride as you did on Ride 7 at the park office. Go right on the gravel road.

0.2 Take a right onto a wide, grassy trail directly across from the turn you made on the previous trail. Trail is in better overall condition for bikes on this side, and there are not as many mosquitoes! These are great cross-country ski trails; be sure to come back and try them out.

1.1 Go right at the fork and reach the gravel road. Turn right again and head back to the start.

1.3 Trailhead. Short and sweet.

Louisville Swamp

Location: Between Shakopee and Jordan on the river side of U.S Highway 169.

Distance: 3 separate loops; 2–4.5 miles. Combine loops for a longer excursion.

Time: 35–60 minutes, depending on how long you spend feeling historical.

Tread: Hard-packed gravel, grass, and dirt singletrack and doubletrack.

Aerobic level: Moderate.

• Louisville Swamp Trail

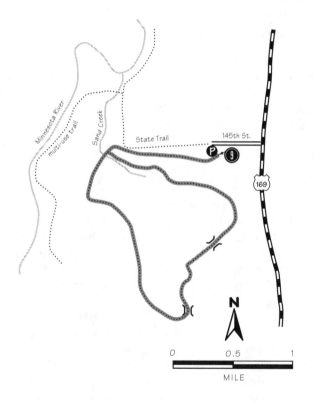

Minnesota River

multi-use trail

Sand Creek

State Trail

145th St.

P 9

169

N

0   0.5   1

MILE

Technical difficulty: 2–3, with nasty bumpy stretch on Little Prairie Loop.

Hazards: Loose gravel and rocks; mud and water on trail; easy to ride off on the wrong trail; big swamp—lots o' big mosquitoes (bring Bug-Be-Gone).

Highlights: One of the most historic areas in the river valley; uncrowded.

Land status: U.S. Fish and Wildlife Service.

Maps: Trail brochure at trailhead or refuge office.

Access: Trailhead is approximately 3.5 miles south of Shakopee on US 169. Turn right from US 169 at 145th Street (sign for Louisville Swamp). Proceed across railroad tracks and into parking lot on the left.

The ride

0.0 Ride to south end of parking lot to information kiosk. Read interesting historical notes on the area and proceed on the hard-packed gravel trail. Ride past the gate and onto the Little Prairie Loop Trail. Here you will find an extremely bumpy section of trail, so bad it is nearly unridable. It is short-lived, however, as you ride along to . . .

0.4 A native oak savanna ecosystem currently being restored. Be sure to look around at this rare natural environment.

1.0 Junction with State Corridor Trail; turn left. Here you have the option to complete the Little Prairie Loop or continue. Let's keep riding. Head down the Corridor Trail and a gradual descent with loose rocks and gravel. Don't let your bike slip out from under you.

1.2 Junction with Mazomani Trail. Mazomani was the chief of a Dakota Indian tribe that called this area home. Turn left into the woods. God help you if you linger too long at any stop; these mosquitoes aren't of this earth. Only your bike will remain. Enjoy good views of Sand Creek shortly after entering the forest.

1.8 Lean to the right and down a long, gradual descent into thick undergrowth, nettles, and other swamp foliage. Trail is really skinny through here. The Louisville Swamp itself is to your right (it seems like you're riding right through the swamp).

2.5 Take the right fork at this junction and ride past the Ehmiller homestead and down into bottomland forest.

3.1 Cross a wooden bridge onto a forested island in the swamp. Follow the trail across a second bridge and return to higher ground near a big ol' glacial boulder, where you will make a right turn and follow the edge of the bluff for about 1 mile.

4.2 Here you are at the Jabs Farm. Stop and be quiet. You can't help feeling the past and imagining life in days gone by. Ride/walk carefully across a rocky section over Sand Creek and up the hill on the other side. Water is available from a pump a short ride to the left before climbing the hill. Continue 0.75 mile to the junction where you started this loop. Stay on the Corridor Trail all the way back to the trailhead.

6.1 Trailhead.

Personal note: This is a very unique and interesting area, and also a fragile one. Riding a bike, I think, is a secondary means to explore the swamp and surrounding forests. The riding is rough and very muddy after a rain. Choose your riding days wisely: stay away from here when it's wet; stay on the marked trails; ride in late fall/early winter when the ground is hard and the shrubbery isn't as aggressive.

Lake Elmo Park Reserve

Location: 1 mile north of Interstate 94 on County Road 19 (Keats Avenue).

Distance: Choose any distance to your liking—8 miles of trail to explore.

Time: 10 minutes to an hour or more.

Tread: A mix of hard-packed singletrack and wide, grassy trail.

Aerobic level: Easy+.

Technical difficulty: 2 on entire trail.

Hazards: Maybe some loose sand or gravel; a tendency to ride off the trail while looking at the abundant wildlife.

Highlights: Rolling terrain through forest and prairie; abundant wildlife; uncrowded trails.

Land status: Washington County Parks.

Maps: Best map is in the park brochure available at the entrance station.

Access: Enter the park 1 mile north of I-94 on Keats Avenue. After parting with $4 for a daily pass at the entrance station (season passes also available), proceed approximately 0.25 mile north to a parking area on the left side of the road.

Lake Elmo Park Reserve Trail

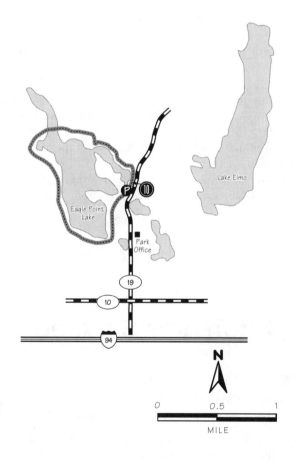

Lake Elmo

Eagle Point Lake

P 10

Park Office

19

10

94

N

0   0.5   1
MILE

The ride

0.0 Trailhead. Trail is shared with hikers and horses. Use caution. There are a variety of options available right from the get-go. On this particular day I did a quick 4-mile loop around Eagle Point Lake and passed several other trails along the way. This area is perfect for exploring. Since there isn't a single trail to follow, just ride! Go left or go right at the trailhead, and then choose one of a dozen different spin-off trails.

Eighty percent of the 3.5 square miles that encompass Lake Elmo Park Reserve are set aside for preservation and/or protection. The prairies and forests of this park will eventually look similar to the way they did prior to the mid-1800s when the first settlers arrived.

Camping, fishing, hiking, horseback riding, and other activities are also available as diversions from your riding.

Afton Alps Ski Area

Location: 21 miles southeast of downtown St. Paul.

Distance: 7 miles of trails available.

Time: Varies; 12 minutes to an hour or more.

Tread: All trails are on dirt singletrack, with some loose gravel thrown in to keep you guessing.

• Afton Alps Ski Area Trail

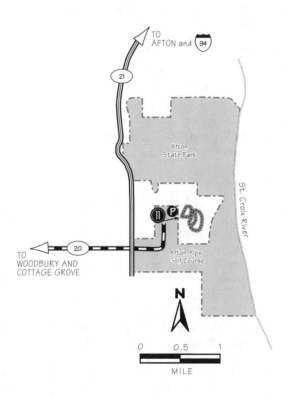

TO
AFTON and 94

21

Afton
State Park

St. Croix River

11 P

TO
WOODBURY AND
COTTAGE GROVE

20

Afton Alps
Golf Course

N

```
0        0.5        1
▮▮▮▮▮▮▮▮▮▮▮▮▮▮▮▮▮▮▮▮▮
        MILE
```

Aerobic level: Strenuous.

Technical difficulty: Consistent 3+ and 4; with a couple sections of –5.

Hazards: Loose rocks; steep descents with sharp turns; super-bumpy cross trails on ski runs.

Highlights: Spectacular scenery in the St. Croix Valley; leg-bustin' climbs (this could also be labeled a hazard); hair-raising descents.

Land status: Afton Alps is a privately owned ski area.

Maps: Best maps available at clubhouse at the top of the hill.

Access: Exit Interstate 94 at Manning Avenue and go south 7 miles to Seventieth Street (County Road 20). Head east 3.5 miles to the entrance to Afton Alps Golf Course (located at the top of the ski area). Park at the clubhouse/chalet and go inside to pay the $6 fee and get a trail map.

The ride

0.0 Begin riding on north side of clubhouse. Afton uses red and blue poles in the ground to mark the trails. Keep these on your right. Steep climbs, technical sections of singletrack, and rocky climbs all greet you almost immediately after the start. Trail passes in and out of heavily wooded areas and across grassy ski runs. Use caution on some narrow turns and watch speed on the downhills. Beauteous views of the St. Croix River Valley from the top.

1.1 Descend a steep hill and pass a pond on your left, leading to a medium-length climb with loose gravel at the start. Kinda cool to stop and listen to the silence at the base of the hill. Chair lifts rest quietly above you, waiting for the excited activity of winter skiers.

1.4 Enjoy a long, gradual descent with some sections of loose gravel. Take a hard left at the bottom onto a rocky part of the path, then slowly grind back up the hill, following the trail to the clubhouse.

2.1 Clubhouse and trailhead. This loop is just one of many at Afton. Explore the hill and challenge yourself on steep climbs and rocky downhills.

Battle Creek Regional Park

Location: Between Upper and Lower Afton roads on the eastern fringes of St. Paul.

Distance: Varies; 1 mile or 10 depending on your mood.

Time: 10 minutes to 2 hours.

Tread: Entire loop is on hard-packed singletrack.

Aerobic level: Moderate+ to strenuous.

Technical difficulty: 3–4.

Hazards: Steep, high-speed downhills; narrow trails with sharp turns; some loose dirt and rocks.

Highlights: Rolling, rollicking trails through thick woods; deer aplenty; lots of different choices of loops to ride.

Land status: Ramsey County.

Maps: County maps.

• Battle Creek Regional Park Trail

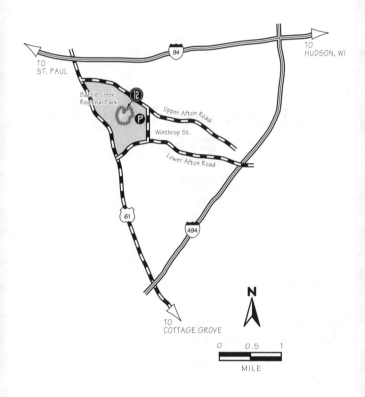

Access: From U.S. Highway 61, take Upper or Lower Afton Road to Winthrop Street and proceed to park entrance. Follow trail signs to fun!

The ride

0.0   Head for the hills on wide ski trails, climbing up toward the woods.

Pick a path and go. I did a nice little 4-mile loop clockwise around the park. There are numerous side trails all over the place. Explore like crazy and enjoy steep ups and downs, diverse tread types, and lots o' wildlife. Watch for other riders and be ready for greasy conditions after a rain.

Terrace Oaks

Location: Directly north of Interstate 35 East, west of County Road 11 in Burnsville.

Distance: 2.9-mile loop.

Time: 15–25 minutes.

Tread: Entire loop is mix of gravel and dirt singletrack.

Aerobic level: Moderate+.

Technical difficulty: 2–3+, with an expert section of 4.

• Terrace Oaks Trail

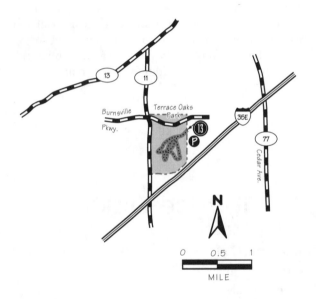

Hazards: Tight, sharp turns; steep climbs with rocks and roots; fast descents with loose gravel.

Highlights: All of the above; fun, challenging ride in remote setting within the city; great place to test your bike handling skills.

Land status: City of Burnsville.

Maps: Map available at trailhead.

Access: Go north approximately 1 mile from I-35 East to Burnsville Parkway. Turn left to park entrance (first right turn). Or take Minnesota 13 east from I-35 West to County Road 11. *Note: Mountain bikes not allowed at west entrance on CR 11.*

The ride

0.0 Ride from the trailhead past hockey rink and into the woods. Do not ride on the hiking trail. A couple of short, steep climbs greet you almost immediately, then the trail deposits you onto some tight, twisting turns. Try to keep your bar ends and hands from shaving the bark off passing trees.

1.1 A steep drop takes you quickly through an open area, passing a pond on the left and the cut-off trail on your right. Get ready for a tough hump up another technical climb.

1.4 Long, gradual descent. Be alert for loose gravel. Trail takes a hard left at the top of a small knoll and becomes more rocky. A side trip for experts branches off to the left on the descent. Enjoy some looooong, speedy downhills as the trail makes its way back to the start.

2.9 Trailhead. Just getting warmed up? Let's go again!

Lebanon Hills Regional Park

Location: Approximately 0.5 mile southeast of junction of Cliff Road and Interstate 35 East in Eagan.

Distance: 2.3-mile loop.

Time: 10–20 minutes.

Tread: Entire loop is mix of gravel and dirt singletrack.

Aerobic level: Strenuous.

Technical difficulty: 2 at beginning and end; 3–4+ on rest of loop.

Hazards: One fast descent with a sharp turn on loose turf; steep climbs on loose, rocky ground; some erosion gullies to look out for.

Highlights: Again, the hazards are the highlights: the climbs are tough but are rewarded with a flyer down a ravine resembling a bobsled course with banked turns and all. Woo hoo!

Land status: Dakota County Parks.

Maps: Map at trailhead.

Access: Go east on Cliff Road 0.5 mile from I-35 East to Johnny Cake Ridge Road. Turn right for another 0.5 mile to park entrance.

• Lebanon Hills Regional Park Trail

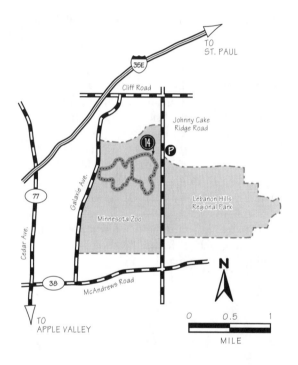

The ride

Note: For this ride all mileage points are approximate.

0.0 Begin riding this counterclockwise loop at the west end of the parking area. Trail starts out wide and gravelly, heading up a medium climb. A spur to the left sneaks through the woods for a shorter loop.

0.8 After turning to dirt singletrack, the trail drops down a steep hill and makes a sharp left turn at the bottom. Use caution so you don't lose it and end up in a heap out on the centerline on Galaxie Avenue.

1.4 A short meander through the trees takes you to the first steep hill. Grunt up and through the loose rocks and dirt, suck wind for a brief minute, then go again at another climb tougher than its predecessor.

1.7 Finally, after crushing your quads, hold on for the steepest and most thrilling ride so far. A long descent sends you through gentle turns with sloped banks where you can lean the bike down and blast out for the straight-away.

2.3 After catching your breath, a few more uphill strokes bring you back to the trailhead. This trail is made for multiple laps—gotta have a go at that hill again!

Elm Creek Park Reserve

Location: 3 miles north of interchange of the Interstate 494/94/694 bedlam.

Distance: 5-mile loop.

Time: 15–30 minutes.

Tread: 1 mile paved trail; 4 miles dirt and grass single and doubletrack.

Aerobic level: Easy.

Technical difficulty: 1 on paved trail; 1–2 on dirt sections.

Hazards: Virtually none. Some bumpy sections keep you guessing, and the handsome scenery tends to avert your eyes from the trail.

Highlights: Great beginner loop in Hennepin County's largest park; fun paved path and nature center available for diversions from the dirt; lots of wildlife.

Land status: Hennepin Parks.

Maps: Park maps available at visitor center.

Access: From U.S. Highway 169 and I-94/694, go north approximately 2 miles to County Road 81. Turn left and take CR 81 2.5 miles to Territorial Road. Go right to the park entrance. Pay $4 daily fee.

• Elm Creek Park Reserve Trail

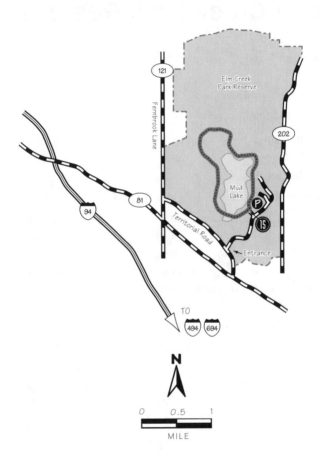

The ride

0.0 Trailhead at visitor center. Follow signs behind building onto the path. Fantabulous scenery right off the bat. After an initial glide downhill, enjoy the sights and sounds of the wetland area filtering into Mud Lake. A wooden boardwalk carries you to dry land on the other side. Suggestion: get off your bike and walk through here; the place is teeming with waterfowl and other wildlife. I scared off a big blue heron and a flock of mallards in the first 10 feet. Make your way across stealthily and you're sure to see all kinds of critters.

0.8 Great views of Mud Lake at the top of a little climb, and an excellent place to watch the sun come up. Cross paved bike path shortly after and continue on the dirt trail.

1.9 At the top of a short, steep little climb, hang a left on the paved path to continue your clockwise loop. Ride for just a couple of pedal strokes and drop back onto the path, which turns to mostly grass. Really bumpy through this section. When I ride this trail again, I'll take the paved trail and skip the human jackhammer session. Follow the well-marked trails back to the start.

4.4 Trailhead. There are close to 20 miles of paved bike/hike trails at Elm Creek. Try some out to see more of this wonderful park.

16

Lake Rebecca Park Reserve

Location: Approximately 30 miles west of Minneapolis on County Road 50, directly south of small burg of Rockford.

Distance: 3.8-mile loop.

Time: 15–25 minutes.

Tread: Entire loop is oh-so-sweet packed singletrack.

Aerobic level: Moderate+.

Technical difficulty: 2–3 on whole loop.

Hazards: A little loose gravel near bottom of some hills; potential crash at a paved trail crossing.

Highlights: One of the prettiest rides in this book and my favorite, especially in the fall and early in the morning; uncrowded, quiet; excellent trail condition over rolling hills with few technical sections; flying turns, quick descents, challenging climbs; a straight-up ideal mountain bike loop.

Land status: Hennepin Parks.

Maps: Park map available from main office or entrance station.

Access: From Minneapolis, take Minnesota 55 west to CR 50 at the outskirts of Rockford; turn left and follow road to park entrance. Pay $4 daily fee and follow signs to mountain bike trailhead.

• Lake Rebecca Park Reserve

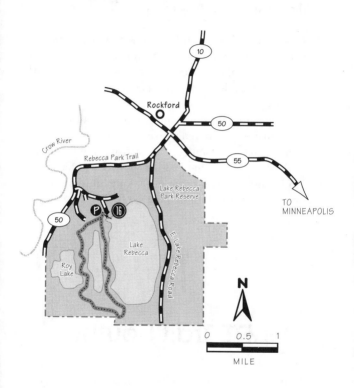

Rockford

Crow River

Rebecca Park Trail

Lake Rebecca Park Reserve

10

50

55

TO MINNEAPOLIS

50

P · 16

Lake Rebecca

Roy Lake

E. Lake Rebecca Road

N

0   0.5   1

MILE

The ride

0.0 Trail begins at south end of parking/boat ramp area. Phone available at start. Enjoy a nice warm-up climb through dense woods. Great views of open meadow and nearby ponds.

0.9 Cross paved bike path here and stretch your legs on another good hill. At the top, stop and enjoy a fantastic view of Lake Rebecca (here's to ya, Bec!) and the "skyline" of Rockford—just a couple of water towers. Great spot for a picnic.

1.8 Pick up some speed on a long downhill but BEWARE: you will cross the paved path again quickly; use caution to avoid plowing someone over. Continue on the dirt trail over more rolling and heavily-wooded terrain.

3.8 Trailhead. Can you resist not taking another lap? Or how about the 6.5 miles of paved trail? Enjoy!

LRT Trail South

Location: Trailhead is a half-mile south of Minnesota Highway 5 on County Road 4 at junction with Scenic Heights Road in Eden Prairie.

Distance: 9 miles, out and back.

Time: 45–60 minutes.

Tread: Entire ride is on hard-packed limestone path.

• LRT Trail South

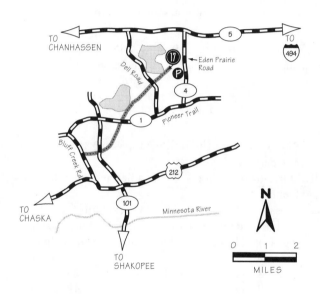

TO
CHANHASSEN

TO
494

Dell Road

17

← Eden Prairie
Road

P

4

5

1

Pioneer Trail

Bluff Creek Rd.

212

TO
CHASKA

101

Minnesota River

TO
SHAKOPEE

N

0   1   2

MILES

Aerobic level: Easy.

Technical difficulty: 1 on whole trail.

Hazards: Use caution when crossing roads.

Highlights: Excellent cruise on old rail line with nice views of the river valley; gradual descent on way down, a little push on the way back; perfect route for all abilities.

Land status: Hennepin Parks.

Maps: Hennepin Parks offers a convenient map of these trails.

Access: Start at Eden Prairie Road (CR 4) and Scenic Heights Road and ride southwest on the wide gravel trail.

The ride

0.0 Ride west from the trailhead, passing the exclusive Bearpath neighborhood.

2.0 Skirt southern shores of Lake Riley and carefully cross Pioneer Trail.

3.2 Cross over MN 101 and Bluff Creek. Bluff Creek Drive is a fun road for a side trip with a steep grade and winding curves, but only go for it during off-traffic hours.

4.5 Trail ends at U.S. Highway 212. You can continue into Chaska along the highway (wide shoulders) for a snack or just head back. Connecting to County Road 11 in Chaska will send you out to the LRT North Trail.

9.0 Back at the trailhead.

Minnesota Valley State Trail

(Eastern Terminus)

Location: Trail starts at Memorial Park on Minnesota Highway 101 directly east of Shakopee.

Distance: 9.4 miles, out and back.

Time: 35–45 minutes.

Tread: All 9 miles are on paved bike trail.

Aerobic level: Easy.

Technical difficulty: 1 the entire way.

Hazards: Watch for oncoming riders on two sharp turns; trail will flood after heavy rain.

Highlights: Easy terrain along scenic river trail; nice trail to cruise and view wildlife.

Land status: U.S. Fish and Wildlife Service; City of Shakopee.

Maps: Refuge maps (available at refuge headquarters).

Access: Start at Memorial Park just east of Shakopee. Ride to northeast end of park and cross a short bridge onto the paved trail.

• Minnesota Valley State Trail (Eastern Terminus)

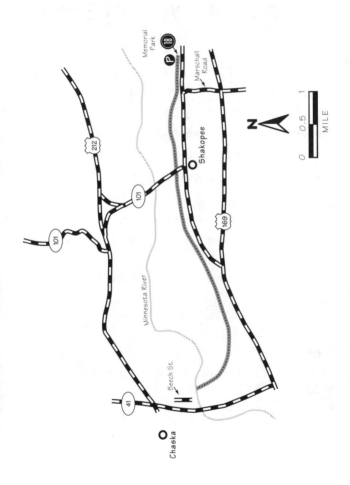

0.0 Ride across the bridge and head west on paved trail. You pass through an RV campground shortly after the start. Be careful not to plow someone down or get squashed by a camper. Continue riding past downtown Shakopee, dropping down through lower river flats and back up on to higher ground with nice views of the valley.

4.7 This is where an old swing bridge waited to whisk you to the other side of the river and on in to Chaska. Presently it is long gone and your ride west abruptly ends here. We hope to see a new bridge built soon. The main stretch of the State Trail shoots off here and offers lots of miles if you're up to it, clear to Belle Plaine. Save that for another day and turn back toward Shakopee.

9.4 Back to the trailhead.

Minnesota Valley— Wilkie Trail

Location: 1 mile west of U.S. Highway 169 on Minnesota 101, south side of Minnesota River.

Distance: 4.3 miles, out and back.

Time: 20–25 minutes.

Tread: 0.75 mile gravel doubletrack; the rest of the trail is grassy singletrack.

• Minnesota Valley–
Wilkie Trail

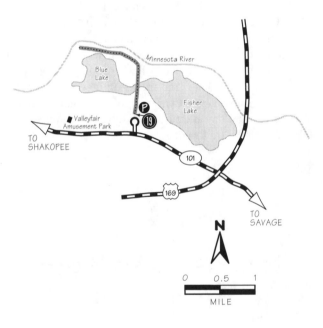

Aerobic level: Easy+.

Technical difficulty: 1–2.

Hazards: Perpetual bumps on grassy portions of trail; hidden ruts to toss you over your bars.

Highlights: Flat terrain good for beginners or an easy ride along the river; wildlife aplenty; uncrowded; otherwise, this trail ranks pretty low on the fun meter.

Land status: U.S. Fish and Wildlife Service.

Maps: Park brochures available at refuge office and (maybe) at trailhead.

Access: Go west from US 169 on MN 101 through one stoplight, then turn right on narrow gravel road at refuge sign.

The ride

0.0 Ride past information kiosk onto gravel doubletrack.

0.8 Reach the riverbank here. Turn left. Trail turns grassy and bumpy. Do not enter this trail during dates listed on sign—herons frequent the area to nest.

2.5 Trail turns left into the woods, but don't do it, the path fizzles out. You'll have to turn around here and head back.

5.2 Back at trailhead.

Cannon Valley Trail

Location: Trailhead for this ride is 3 miles south of U.S. Highway 61 on County Road 7, directly south of the Cannon River from the town of Welch.

Distance: 20 miles, out and back.

Time: 1.25 to 1.5 hours, with more miles available.

Tread: Entire ride is on paved trail.

Aerobic level: Easy; moderate with higher distances.

Technical difficulty: 1 on entire trail.

Hazards: Crowded on weekends; use caution when crossing roads.

Highlights: Excellent ride through high river bluffs; great fall color route; easy access; superb trail conditions.

Land status: Joint ownership—Red Wing, Wisconsin; Cannon Falls, Minnesota; and Goodhue County.

Maps: Best map is available at pay stations at trailheads.

Access: This trail can be reached in Cannon Falls, Red Wing, and Welch. Our ride begins at the Welch station, 0.25 mile south of the little town of the same name. Ample parking is available off CR 7, but fills up fast on sunny weekend days.

• Cannon Valley Trail

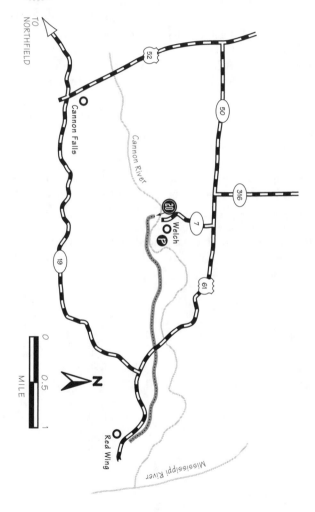

The ride

0.0 Pay $2 daily Wheel Pass (or $10 for the year) and begin riding east toward Red Wing. Shortly after the start you'll ride past Welch Village Ski Area. Take in the sights of rugged bluffs on both sides of the trail. Great views in the fall.

1.5 Ride over Belle Creek on one of many wooden bridges. The next few miles offer good chances to spot all sorts of wildlife both on the ground and in the air.

4.6 Picturesque pastureland to your right with ponds and streams and cows.

5.1 Pass underneath US 61.

10.0 Trail ends at the outskirts of downtown Red Wing. Signs are posted to take you to this charming town. Plan on spending some time there soaking up the atmosphere. Your return to Welch will be slightly uphill, but it's nothing you can't handle.

20.0 Trailhead. Pack up and head over to the General Store in Welch to cool down with some ice cream and other goodies.

Murphy-Hanrehan Park

Location: 3 miles east of Prior Lake at the southern reaches of Savage.

Distance: 6-mile loop.

Time: 30–40 minutes.

Tread: Entire loop is hard-packed singletrack, with some loose gravel thrown in for a little flavor.

Aerobic level: Strenuous.

Technical difficulty: 3+ to 5 on whole loop.

Hazards: Loose gravel and rocks on climbs; high-speed downhills over changing terrain; lack of oxygen as you battle gravity on severe steeps.

Highlights: Extremely challenging loop with constant tough climbs and raging descents; quiet loop through scenic, un-crowded park.

Land status: Hennepin Parks.

Maps: Trail map at entrance station.

Access: From Interstate 35 and County Road 42, go west on CR 42 to Burnsville Parkway. Turn left (south) and go 2 miles to Murphy Lake Road (County Road 75). Turn left and enter park (pay $4 fee at the gate). Phone available at trailhead.

• Murphy-Hanrehan
Park Trail

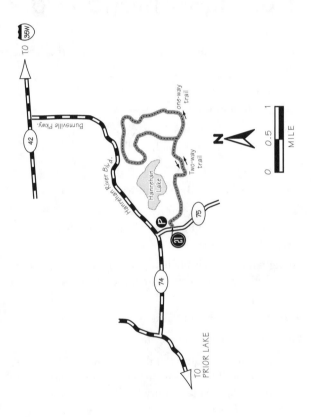

The ride

0.0 Ride past park building onto singletrack trail. Trail is two-way at the start; use caution. Glide over some rollers and a nice warm-up hill at 0.6 mile.

1.2 Ride past peaceful little pond to right of trail.

1.6 Begin one-way trail here along with a steep descent with loose sand at the bottom, followed by a long, very steep climb. Trail rises in tiers, getting progressively tougher the closer you get to the top. Be ready to granny-gear this one. Be rewarded for your effort with a long, fast downhill; be careful. From here on out you will be treated to relentless changes in elevation with steep, technical ups and downs and no chance to enjoy the scenery. This is a serious ride to beef up your hill-climbing skills or punish your riding partner. Come prepared to hammer.

5.8 Trailhead.

Appendix A

Other Area Routes

Here is a short inventory of additional rides that may spin your wheels. These routes all follow paved or gravel off-road paths and are excellent for all riders. To be sure what trail you're on and where it's headed, pick up or send for any number of county, city, or state maps. Most area Chamber of Commerce offices will have available some form of information on the major bike trails. Although it's difficult to get lost on these rides, plan ahead and ride with a partner or inform someone of your expected route.

North Hennepin Regional Trail—A nice cruise along flat terrain between Coon Rapids and Elm Creek Parks. 14 miles round trip with bonus miles at each park. Great for families or beginners.

Luce Line State Trail—Nearly 70 miles of trail here if you can spend a whole day in the saddle. Enjoy a mix of paved and gravel riding on an old rail bed. Terrain is rolling to flat with forests and farms. Check with the Minnesota Department of Natural Resources for current maps and choose your favorite section.

Gateway State Trail—Some of the best paved trail riding around. Again, numerous starting points are available for your choice of mileage. This trail begins in St. Paul and leads to Stillwater with a connection to Duluth on the Munger Trail. Great for families; can get crowded. DNR will have maps and information.

Don't forget about the splendiferous riding along the Mississippi River from Highway 5 to the University of Minnesota and Crosby Farm Park in St. Paul.

Appendix B

Information Sources

Minnesota Valley National Wildlife Refuge—U.S. Fish & Wildlife Service
3815 E. 80th Street
Bloomington, MN 55425
612-335-2323

Minnesota Department of Natural Resources
500 Lafayette Road
St. Paul, MN 55155-4002
650-596-6157
State Parks & Rec.
 651-296-9223
Trail & Waterways
 651-597-1151
Ft. Snelling State Park
 651-725-2389
MN Valley State Trail
 651-492-6400

Ramsey County Parks & Recreation
2015 Van Dyke Street
Maplewood, MN 55109
651-777-1707

Hennepin County Parks
12615 County Road 9
Plymouth, MN 55441
612-559-9000

Washington County Parks
1515 Keats Avenue North
Lake Elmo, MN 55042
651-731-3851

Dakota County Parks
8500 127th Street E
Hastings, MN 55033
651-438-4660

City of St. Paul Parks & Recreation
25 W. 4th St., #300
St. Paul, MN 55102
650-566-6400

City of Burnsville Parks & Recreation
100 Civic Center Pkwy.
Burnsville, MN 55337
612-895-4500

Bike Shops

The Twin Cities area has an excellent selection of bicycle shops. Peruse a local directory to find one near you. Some names to watch for:

Erik's Bike & Fitness
6 locations
612-861-3011

Freewheel Bike
Minneapolis
612-339-2219

Grand Performance
St. Paul
651-699-2640

Bennett's Cycle
St. Louis Park
612-922-0311

Penn Cycle
5 locations
612-866-7540

A Short Index of Rides

This index lists seven different prominent features of area rides. Each ride appears somewhere in this index (some more than once) to allow you to associate a particular trip with what you can expect on the trail.

Paved Paths

18. Minnesota Valley State Trail
20. Cannon Valley Trail
    Also North Hennepin Trail and sections of Luce Line trail.

Sweet Singletrack Rides

3. River Valley Rover
5. Bloomington Ferry Trail
10. Afton Alps
11. Battle Creek Regional Park
12. Terrace Oaks Park
13. Lebanon Hills Regional Park
15. Lake Rebecca Park Reserve
21. Murphy-Hanrehan Park

First Timers

1. Mendota Trail
2. Ft. Snelling State Park
4. Bass Ponds
6. New Bridge Trail
7. St. Lawrence Unit
9. Lake Elmo Park Reserve
14. Elm Creek Park Reserve
16. LRT Trail
17. Minnesota Valley State Trail
20. Cannon Valley Trail

Technical Tests
3. River Valley Rover
5. Bloomington Ferry Trail
10. Afton Alps
12. Terrace Oaks Park
21. Murphy-Hanrehan Park

Deep in the Woods (as deep as you can be in an urban setting)
3. River Valley Rover
5. Bloomington Ferry Trail
7. St. Lawrence Unit
8. Louisville Swamp
11. Battle Creek Regional Park
12. Terrace Oaks Park
15. Lake Rebecca Park Reserve
21. Murphy-Hanrehan Park

The Flats
1. Mendota Trail
2. Fort Snelling State Park
16. LRT Trail
17. Minnesota Valley State Trail
19. Wilkie Trail
20. Cannon Valley Trail

The Hills
1. Murphy-Hanrehan Park
3. River Valley Rover
10. Afton Alps
11. Battle Creek Regional Park
13. Lebanon Hills Regional Park
15. Lake Rebecca Park Reserve

Glossary

ATB: All-terrain bicycle; a.k.a. mountain bike, fat tire flyer, dirt dog.

Bail: Getting off the bike, usually in a hurry, and many times not by choice. Often a last resort. Also a verb indicating a course of action: "Let's bail after we finish this last climb."

Bunny hop: Leaping up, while riding, and lifting both wheels off the ground to jump over an obstacle (or just for the fun of it).

Clean: To ride without touching a foot (or other body part) to the ground; to ride a tough section successfully.

Contour: A line on a topographic map showing a continuous elevation level over uneven ground. Also a verb indicating a fairly easy or moderate grade: "The trail contours around the western fringe of the ridge."

Downfall: Trees or branches that have fallen across the trail.

Doubletrack: A trail, jeep road, ATV route, or other track with two distinct ribbons of tread, typically with grass growing in between. No matter which side you choose, the other rut always looks smoother.

Endo: Lifting the rear wheel off the ground and riding (or abruptly not riding) on the front wheel only. Also known, at various degrees of control and finality, as a nose wheelie, "going over the bars," and a face plant.

Fall line: The angle and direction of a slope; the **line** you follow when gravity is in control and you aren't.

Hammer: To ride hard; derived from how it feels afterward: "I'm hammered."

Hammerhead: Someone who actually enjoys feeling **hammered**. A Type A rider who goes hard and fast all the time.

Header: See **endo**.

Kelly Hump: An abrupt mound of dirt across the road or trail.

Line: The route (or trajectory) between or over obstacles or through turns. **Tread** or trail refers to the ground you're riding on; the line is the path you choose within the tread (and may only exist in your imagination).

Out-of-the-saddle: Like it reads, hoisting your butt off of the saddle and really stomping on the pedals; commonly done during a sprint or a climb.

Quads: Thigh muscles (short for quadriceps); or maps in the USGS topographic series (short for quadrangles). The right quads (of either kind) can prevent or get you out of trouble in the north woods.

Singletrack: A trail, game run, or other track with only one ribbon of **tread**. A good piece of singletrack is pure fat tire fun.

Spur: A side road or trail that splits off from the main route.

Surf: Riding through loose gravel or sand, when the wheels slalom from side to side. Also *heavy surf*: frequent and difficult obstacles.

Suspension: A bike with front suspension has a shock-absorbing fork or stem. Rear suspension absorbs shock between the rear wheel and frame. A bike with both is said to be fully suspended.

Track stand: Balancing on a bike in one place, without rolling forward appreciably. Cock the front wheel to one side and bring that pedal up to the one or two o'clock position. Now control your side-to-side balance by applying pressure on the pedals and brakes and changing the angle of the front wheel, as needed. It takes practice but really comes in handy at stoplights and when trying to free a foot from your pedal before falling.

Tread: The riding surface, particularly regarding **singletrack.**

Water bar: A log, rock, or other barrier placed in the **tread** to divert water off the trail and prevent erosion. Peeled logs can be slippery and cause bad falls, especially when they angle sharply across the trail.

Whoop-dee-doo: A series of kelly humps used to keep vehicles off trails. Watch your speed or do the dreaded top tube tango.

About the Author

Steve Johnson is the author of another FalconGuide, *Mountain Biking Chequamegon,* which covers rides in north-central Wisconsin. He is a freelance writer and his work has appeared in *Bicycling* magazine and Rocky Mountain National Park's *Trail*. A road racer at heart, he discovered a taste for dirt while attending college in the Colorado mountains. He currently lives with his wife in St. Paul, Minnesota, routinely eluding any threat of responsibility so he can continue to ride.

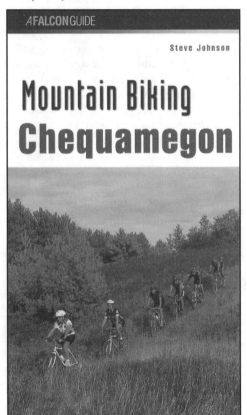